SOCIAL MEDIA MARKETING.

Here Come, 25 New Ideas for Social Media Marketing Using Twitter.

by

Robert Awere

Other books by the publisher **Awere First Publishing** can be seen on https://www.awerefirstpublishing.com, or check on our book list. OR on, **https://amzn.to/2FEN65j**

Also, you can follow us on our various **Social Media Platforms**:

- **PINTEREST**: kindlebooks8566
- **YOUTUBE**: AwereFirstPublishing CHANNEL
- **LINKEDIN**: linkedin.com/in/awerefirst-publishing-26870417b
- **TWITTER**: https://twitter.com/Awerefirstpubl1
- **SOUNDCLOUD** (audiobook samples): www.soundcloud.com/awerefirstpublishing

Table of Contents

Introduction

I want to thank you and congratulate you for downloading the book ***"Social Media Marketing: Here Come 25 New Ideas for Social Media Marketing Using Twitter"***.

If you have ever thought that Twitter was just a tool for those who have a lot of time on their hands, I want you to think again. Twitter can be a potent tool for businesses to reach out to their target audience and engage with potential customers.

It has been reported that Twitter receives over 320 million visitors a month. It is used by a large community of people to express their opinions and experiences with each other. It is an excellent forum to find out what users are saying about your products, and this alone makes it evident just how useful it can be for marketing.

Twitter can be used for posting updates on company products and other events. Once Twitter etiquette and lingo is mastered, it can be an excellent way to reach out to your target audience. It's not difficult to grab the attention of your readers in 280 characters.

Despite Twitter's relative ease of use, there are certain rules you need to play by. For instance, you need to make sure the tweets that you post have a personal tone because that is what people look for in social media sites. Social media users will not tolerate blatant promotional content. If they wanted advertisements, they would turn on the TV. So you need to make sure that your posts are relevant to your product, but aren't just you "selling" or "marketing".

Twitter is frequently used by companies to post about promotions, sales and other specials. These announcements are similar in a way to breaking news. Many companies also host contests via Twitter. By providing this type of useful and personal content, businesses can become entrenched in the lives of their customers.

Twitter is an excellent tool to give your brand an image and also to engage in social listening. Ever wonder what your users are saying about your company? It's simple with Twitter. This social media platform has a special feature which lets you search for a specific business, conversation topic, or even a name and find out what is being said on the subject.

Since Twitter provides the space for everyday events to become momentous pieces of news, people tweet about almost every aspect of their lives. They tweet about products that they are using. You can search for your business name on the site and find out what people are saying about your products.

Inside this guide, you will discover new social media marketing methods and strategies on how to use Twitter for your business. We'll talk about everything from learning how to establish a good relationship with your followers to giving them near-perfect customer service when they eventually buy from you.

Let's get started!

Chapter 1: What Is Social Media?

Social media is certainly the buzz of today. But what is it, how can you benefit from it, and why do you really care? Glad you asked.

First, let's stress that if you think social media is a fad that's going to disappear, you couldn't be further from the truth. Social media is a phenomenon that is taking the internet by storm and is showing no signs of slowing down.

The question of what social media is can be answered in so many ways—it's everything from communication between friends and loved ones to one of the strongest business platforms on our planet.

For the purpose of this guide, we are going to break down exactly how to use social media as a business platform and, more importantly, how to succeed.

According to Wikipedia, social media refers to the use of web-based and mobile technologies to turn communication into interactive dialogue.

I think that still leaves you asking, "What is social media?". I'll break it down a little more.

Social media refers to a group of sites that allow you to participate. For instance, on some blogs, you can leave comments. This starts off the opportunity to be social. You might find an article with as many as 2500 comments. If you look at the article, you'll likely find several people having arguments or discussions in the comment section.

Next, you'll find sites that let you have discussions more easily. For example, this could be a chat room, where you can have a text conversation in real time with other users. Some of these chat rooms also have a voice, and many support videos. Skype, for example, is a chat software that has become a major online communication company.

But many others specialise in just being social. Facebook offers excellent capability to talk back and forth, but it also has integrated games into it. You can play games with people from around the world and talk while you do it. Flickr and Photobucket offer a somewhat different idea. You can upload photos galore to these sites, and then friends can comment on the photos.

Social media has exploded over the past five years with Facebook, Twitter, Digg, Delicious, and thousands of other websites. These websites are geared toward allowing people from all over the world to communicate within a moment's notice. As social media exploded, websites like Facebook and so many others realised that millions of people were using their platform for business and adapted for those businesses.

Those who were quick to jump on the bandwagon and take the time to understand social media marketing have already taken their businesses miles ahead of the competition. Over the next decade, we can expect social media's role in marketing and business to grow by leaps and bounds.

So how big is social media? It's huge! To give you an idea of how huge, here are some recent stats.

- There are more than 2 billion active users on Facebook.
- There are more than 320 million active users on Twitter.
- There are more than 400 million blogs.
- There are more than 600 million YouTube videos.

Social Media by Characteristics

The best way to understand social media is by grouping by characteristic.

- **Openness**: The majority of social media venues promote leaving comments, voting, sharing information, and removing barriers, making content open to everyone.

- **Connectedness**: Social media thrives on being connected with other people, resources, sites, blogs, etc.

- **Conversation**: Traditional media is one-way communication whereas social media is more of a two-way conversation.

- **Participation**: Social media promotes everyone to contribute and provide feedback. Media and audience blur together.

- **Community**: Social media sees communities quickly sprout up based on common interests.

Basic Forms of Social Media

If you're wondering when we are going to get to the meat and potatoes of social media marketing, we are already on our way. To get the most out of this ebook and the concepts we'll discuss, you need to first understand social media and its components. If this is all rather boring to you, or you already have a solid foundation in social media basics, we encourage you to skip forward to the next chapter.

There are five basic forms of social media. Let's have a look at them.

1. Social Networks

These are sites where people build personal and business web pages and then connect with their friends and/or family to communicate, share content and share photos. There are many social networks, although most of us think of Facebook right away.

2. Forums

Forums came before social media and were an important predecessor that remains important today. These are sites where online discussions take place around a specific hobby, topic, or interest. Information is shared and exchanged, and online communities are built.

3. Blogs

Blogs are a well known and popular form of social media. A blog is like an online journal. It can be personal or business. They can be based on a specific topic such as fashion or real estate, or they can be more like a diary discussing daily events or news. Commenting is often an important feature of blogs.

4. Content Communities

Content communities organise and share based on a specific type of content such as videos or photos. YouTube is the biggest content community. There are others such as Flickr or del.icio.us.

5. Microblogging

Microblogging combines social networking and microblogs, which are the equivalent of little sound bites. It's the perfect way of sharing information for mobile devices. Twitter is an excellent example of microblogging and they are considered the leader in the microblogging arena.

Chapter 2: Social Media and the Distribution of Information

Social media has grown at a phenomenal rate, faster than any other area of the internet. It wasn't that many decades ago that the ability to create content and then distribute it to the masses was limited to those with access to television, radio, and print.

If you wanted a video, you would call a television station, which would have employed thousands of professionals who would create, compose, and bring to air your video. If you wanted print material, you would call up a newspaper or magazine that also had teams of writers and editors who would put together your copy and bring it to print.

The internet opened the door to creating one's own content and distributing that content. But even a decade ago, it was still beyond the technical skills of most people. However, today anyone can create their own content and easily distribute it to the masses. Anyone can take advantage of social media and the powerful marketing tool it presents, whether that's using a blog, Facebook, Twitter, or any number of other social media avenues.

How Social Media Networks Work

Social networks grow and prosper when web surfers find a social media network they want to join, so they sign up, create their profile, and begin to connect with friends, family, coworkers, and contacts. They invite others to join the social network, and those people invite more people, and suddenly the social media network has exploded in popularity.

In our digitally connected world, social media sites like Facebook, Twitter, and YouTube continue to skyrocket in popularity and use. As if those are not enough, according to the website Knowem.com there are more than 590 popular and emerging social networks. Who knew!

With so many choices, entrepreneurs and small business owners are struggling to find the right social platform to focus on, as their time and resources are persistently limited.

Not a week goes by without a client asking me these questions: Which social media platform do you think I should focus on to get more customers? Should I try to conquer all the major social media platforms for my business?

It's not easy for me to say which social media platform you should use to get customers. Just like other marketing opportunities, each social media platform has its pros and cons. Your primary focus needs to be creating a strategy and doing some serious planning to attract more ideal clients to generate income.

Let's take a look at what are considered the top five social media platforms and discover how to use these social media tools for business:

- **Facebook**

With more than two billion users, Facebook has quickly skyrocketed to the position of number one in the social media world. Whether you want to play a game of Scrabble with friends, send a virtual gift, or wish someone a happy birthday, it's as easy as one, two, three. The business side of Facebook is quickly growing too, as more and more companies recognise it for the powerful marketing tool it is.

- **Instagram**

Many companies promote themselves excellently on Instagram by posting original and creative images. Brands that use Instagram are becoming very popular for their interesting visual content and integrating the most popular hashtags in their posts.

- **Twitter**

Twitter is amazing and offers an endless flow of leads to your business. Once you have a blog post or article, you can simply enter the URL into Twitter with a short description and watch the leads come in. There are also various tools that can completely automate this process for you, many of which are free.

- **Pinterest**

When you think of Pinterest, remember the saying "a picture is worth a thousand words"? The idea is you "pin" interesting pictures to your virtual board. If you have a business that relies on the visual effects of pictures, then Pinterest is for you, but you can't get in without an invitation.

- **LinkedIn**

Of the many social network sites, LinkedIn is the one most often used to build professional contacts and grow a business. It has received some disapproval for being too closed to the public and for the fees it charges for some of its services, but it is also the second most popular social network site, next to Facebook.

- **YouTube**

Who wouldn't capitalise on the planet's number one video sharing site for enhanced visibility? The means and avenues for a successful social marketing plan utilising YouTube include:

— Uploading presentations and demonstrating expertise.
— Providing a channel to reflect your brand and enhance engagement.
— Uploading a creative business video detailing your products and services.
— Arranging an interview with an authority figure.

— Vlogging, movie-making and music-sharing enable businesses to promote their offers on YouTube.

- **Blog**

When we ask what is social media, blogging is the single most important part of any online business working within social media. I have various articles that show you how to set up a blog within two hours. It is not difficult at all.

A blog becomes your central hub for your business that prospects will visit often if it's set up correctly. If you implement the correct search engine optimisation strategies from the start, your blog will generate leads for the rest of your life.

The One Thing to Remember

Really, the point of social media is participation. You could just as easily call these sites participation sites.

You use them to interact with other people. You can post websites you like to Stumbleupon, news you like to Digg, videos you like to YouTube, or start a new personal blog at LiveJournal or Blogspot. And at every one of these sites, you can comment on everybody else's stuff. It makes the web a community, a place to get to know people or at least to share views. You can take that to another level if you want, or remain anonymous behind your screen name. It's up to you.

You can also build a business through these same sites, by sharing what you know through your sites and leading people to try solutions—products for sale—that will help them. For each sale, you can earn a fee. If you can contact all of them at once and tell them when a new product to help them comes out, you can do quite well.

Social media is a tremendous platform to start a business. Like any business in this world, you need a daily strategy that will help you to accomplish your goals. However, please be careful. So many people want to sell you programs online that will not get the job done.

Chapter 3: Social Media Marketing

Social media marketing, often referred to as SMM, is a type of internet marketing that focuses on branding to create product and brand recognition, and creating marketing strategies using the various social media networks that are available. Social media describes the activities that occur, including posting photos, videos, and content, and engaging in social interaction.

It's easy to get so excited over the technology and the internet that sometimes we fail to plan or create the necessary roadmap for your online business to be successful. Social media marketing is a powerful tool that can aid your business in reaching its highest goals.

SMM, the new tool in the business arena, has shown a promising rise in recent years. The web world is going gaga over it and social media has shown a 100 percent higher lead-to-close rate than outbound marketing. Today, nearly 84 percent of business-to-business (B2B) marketers use social media in some form or another. No matter what you sell and who your target audience is, using social media as a marketing tool is a sure-shot way to grow your brand!

Importance of Social Media Marketing

Not having an active social media presence is kind of like living in ancient times. People may ask, "What is social media marketing going to do for me? Do I really need it?" Yes. Yes, you do. Just check out the reasons why:

- **Increased Web Traffic**

Social media posts can drive targeted traffic. Creating a new page on your site, landing pages, and well-placed social media posts can make all the difference. A single link on Reddit or links submitted to StumbleUpon can transform a page from a handful of visitors a day to hundreds. Who wouldn't want to capitalise on that?

- **Boost SEO**

Social media can boost your site's search engine optimisation (SEO). Search engine crawlers know which pages are consistently earning traffic and which are just floating out there, forgotten and ignored. Driving traffic to your optimised pages with social media posts will cause them to climb much faster in the search engine results pages (SERPs).

- **Connect with Consumers and Industry Leaders**

Social media leads to real relationship-building. Twitter and Instagram marketing can get you free interaction with your customer base—you can read their tweets and status updates to get insights into their daily lives, like what products they prefer and why, etc. With this information, maybe you can fine-tune your strategy.

You can also use social media as a tool to connect with thought leaders and tastemakers in your space, as well as journalists who cover your industry.

- **Get Your Message Across**

As people view Twitter and Facebook as social networks, not marketing machines, they're less likely to see what you post as marketing and will be more likely to hear what you have to say. This translates to serious web traffic when you link to your site and posts that market themselves as your friends and followers share what you've posted.

- **Targeting and Retargeting with Ads**

The highly customisable nature of social media ads, like Facebook ads, is one of the reasons social media is important. These ads even allow you to target users by things like location, education level, industry, and even purchase history and the pages they've liked. You also have the option to retarget the users who visit you and even convert them into solid leads and sales.

- **Get Noticed at Events**

It's easier to get noticed at events and even generate earned media coverage with social media posts. At any event, there's no better way to leverage your presence than with the help of social media.

- **Immediate response**

The feedback you get in the process of SMM means you'll be the first to know when there are issues ... and you can take immediate steps to resolve them right away. Consumers appreciate companies that respond quickly to customer complaints.

- **Builds Brand Loyalty**

Brand loyalty can be built on a strong social media presence. It has been found that brands with active social media profiles have more loyal customers. Being active on social media helps you become less like a business and more like what you truly are: a unified group of people who share a vision.

How to Create Activity With Social Media

The internet lets you interact with web surfers and you can create and promote your content by using the right strategy. You can reach targeted traffic and key influencers with social media. Let's look at some important tips that can help you get a better understanding of social media marketing.

- **Process:** Don't become a follower trying to keep up with every idea that comes along. Instead, set your goals and establish your own processes, such as keyword research or content analysis, then map out your plan. Far too many companies will move too fast before they've ever put a plan in place. If you don't put a plan into place, you are not going to see any good results.

- **Assistance:** When it comes to social media, helping others is a key to success. People fail with their social media marketing because they are too about "me," and not enough about "them." Always remember that your efforts should be about those who are visiting your social media marketing page, not about you.

- **Connect:** You can reach out to those who are influencers in the marketplace. You'll be surprised how brand advocates can help you in your niche. Remember to always be polite and sincere.

- **Contribute:** You need to create content that is of the highest quality. As important as social media is, content remains the most important aspect of your online business and marketing campaign. There are a number of opportunities waiting for you.

- **Position Yourself:** To create a powerful connection to your brand and your company, learn how to position yourself amongst consumer passion.

- **Blog:** A blog is so easy to set up, and it is one of the most powerful social media tools out there. As more and more people discover their value, they begin to grow at an astronomical rate.

- **Links:** Don't be afraid of linking. Linking to other websites and blogs can be a powerful tool for you to build a targeted audience. Search engines are built on links. Learn how to use them to your advantage to drive traffic to your website.

- **Videos:** Video is one of the fastest growing sectors of the internet. You have the potential to reach millions when you use video correctly. For a wider distribution there are other tools that you can use such as vidmetrix.com to aid in automating distribution of your videos. You'll draw the most viewers with videos that are funny, weird, and controversial in nature.

- **RSS Feeds:** RSS feeds are an excellent way to spread the word. You can easily distribute update notices, headlines, and content changes. People like to be kept in the loop and know what's going on. Subscribing to an RSS feed allows them to do that. There are all kinds of RSS feeds that people subscribe to including My Yahoo Web and iGoogle, as well as many others. Make sure you take advantage of what an RSS feed can do for you.

- **Micro-Communities:** There are all kinds of micro-communities that pertain to your business. In fact, there's a micro-community for almost every interest. For example, gardenweb.com, education.com, shoetube.com, etc. If you want to have your voice heard, micro-communities are a much better option than trying to get noticed on one of the large communities such as Digg.com. Create relevant remarks that are linkworthy, and don't forget to connect with the top influencers online.

Chapter 4: Defining Your Audience on Social Media

If you want to get the most out of your social media marketing, you must understand your audience. Social media has evolved into far more than just an interesting site that people use to chat about their day-to-day lives. Many social media sites, like Facebook, have become virtual communities where friends interact, new friends are made, awareness campaigns occur, games are played, and much, much more. Business has been slow to recognise just how powerful social media is.

Just recently, more businesses have recognised there is a huge untapped market here with the potential to skyrocket their sales to a new level. By developing solid marketing strategies to use with social media you can also enjoy the benefits.

Don't make the mistake of thinking that if you build it, they will come. That's simply not the way it is. Too many businesses quickly throw up a website, start a blog, sign up to Twitter and start tweeting, and create a business page at Facebook, then they sit back in anticipation and are distraught when they reap no benefits, wondering what they did wrong.

Here's what you need to do to enjoy successful social media marketing.

1. Create a Profile

Don't create a profile for a single person. A better strategy is to create a profile that is a representative character for thousands, even millions of individuals that will connect to your business using social media channels.

2. What to Look For

If you want to understand your social media persona, look to those who are already connected to you. To build a strong persona, ask these three key questions:

- What are the content preferences of your customers?
- How do they discover content and then consume and/or share that content?
- What are they looking to discuss on the social web?

Once you have the answers to these questions, you can make smart decisions about what your content should be, and how to best present it.

Targeting Your Audience

The type of business you have is important in targeting your audience with social media. For example, if you own a pet supply store, you will want to find all of the pet owners out there. They are the ones who will be interested in your products and services, and will be the "bread and butter" of your business. Someone looking for comic books isn't going to care that you have a good sale going on for parakeet food or that you are the best dog groomer in your area.

The specifics of getting your business known through social media can be confusing at times, so it is important to start with some general guidelines and dig deeper into more specific audiences later on. After all, you want your business and branding to be on the tip of everyone's tongue in order to capitalise on your share of the market. Once you get a good idea of how social media can help you, targeting specific audiences will be a lot easier. With that being said, let's explore some of the most popular social media sites and some ways you can use them to boost your business.

How to Build Your Social Media Profile

There are all kinds of sites popping up that offer services to build your customer profile. If you want to undertake this project on your own, you need to keep these three powerful yet simple tools in mind when developing your social media profile.

- **Surveys** – The main reason a business is unable to profile the visitors to their site is because they don't take the time to interact with their visitors. The easiest way to interact with your visitors is to ask questions. Surveys are a great way to ask questions and get answers that can help.

- **Web Analytics** – Google Analytics is one of the most popular analytical tools, and best of all, it's completely free. It's set up in a manner that makes it easy even for beginners. Any business that wants to be successful with their social media understands the profile and uses some type of web analytics.

Rapleaf – There are other sites like this, but Rapleaf is one of the popular choices. Its purpose is to ensure that every person that uses the internet has a meaningful experience. Here's how it works. First, you send Rapleaf a list of all your email addresses for your users. Rapleaf then searches its database for that particular email address and provides you with information about the person associated with that email address, including age, gender, and location.

Chapter 5: Introduction to Twitter

Imagine how many people you are reaching with current updates around the clock, seven days per week, around the world. This site is another popular mobile site that reaches people wherever they are and whenever they are there. Twitter is an extremely popular site that has seen monumental growth in the past few years.

Twitter is a micro-communication tool and platform that combines texting, blogging, emailing, and social networking. By combining these it allows users to reach people they would not be able to reach. It also allows you to stay on top of industry trends and news that interest you as you build your network of friends, family, peers, and industry colleagues.

Twitter has more than 75 million accounts worldwide that connect with each other using 280 characters or less. Messages sent to other users who have opted to follow you are known as a 'tweet'. Twitter includes private and public messages. You can send direct messages, or DMs, privately to your contacts, or public messages '@...topic...' that can be read by anyone interested in the topic.

Revealed below are current Twitter stats, demographics and fun facts, gleaned from Omnicore.

Twitter Statistics

- Total number of monthly active Twitter users: 326 million
- Total number of Tweets sent per day: 500 million
- Percentage of Twitter users on mobile: 80%
- Number of Twitter daily active users: 100 million

Twitter Demographics

- 24% of all internet male users use Twitter, whereas 21% of all internet female users use Twitter.
- There are 261 million international Twitter users. 79% of Twitter accounts are based outside the United States.
- There are over 69 million Twitter users in the U.S.
- Roughly 46% of Twitter users are on the platform daily.
- The total number of Twitter users in the UK is 13 million.
- 37% of Twitter users are between the ages of 18 and 29; 25% users are 30–49 years old.
- 56% of Twitter users earn $50,000 or more in a year.
- The top three countries by user count outside the U.S. are Brazil (27.7 million users), Japan (25.9 million), and Mexico (23.5 million).
- 36% of Americans aged 18 to 29 years old use Twitter.
- 80% of Twitter users access the platform on a mobile device, and 93% of video views are on mobile.

Fun Facts

- Twitter can handle 18 quintillion user accounts.
- 74% of Twitter users say they use the network to get their news.
- 85% of small and medium business users use Twitter to provide customer service.
- More than 100 million tweets contained GIFs in 2015.

- Saudi Arabia has the highest percentage of internet users who are active on Twitter.
- In Q3 2017, Twitter live-streamed more than 830 events.
- Twitter also live-streamed 96 million hours of live user-generated content in Q3 via Periscope.
- Number of Twitter timeline views in 2014 is 200 billion.
- 83% of 193 UN member countries have a Twitter presence.
- Twitter's revenue per employee is $488,913.

With these enormous figures, I'm sure you would agree that Twitter can probably give your business the opportunity to engage with your customers on a daily basis.

Twitter is a social media platform that is being extensively used to generate traffic to blogs and websites. It is also being used to distribute news, stories, political views, sports, entertainment events, and many other subjects that are of general or particular interest.

Twitter is also a marketing tool for companies and businesses that are willing to listen and participate in public conversations to find ways to attract new clients and to turn current ones into loyal customers. Companies can test, get feedback and create buzz about their products and services.

The most active users mostly comprise media, public relations experts and politicians. They are part of a Twitter elite group known as influencers. If you can reach and engage with them, then you have the opportunity to be visible to thousands of users that follow them.

People also use Twitter to find out what others are talking about. In other words, find out what is trending, while having the opportunity to examine profiles, previous posts and data available through the network.

Twitter Account Basics

The first step in using Twitter is to sign up. Signing up is very easy. The first thing you have to do is choose a username. Your username should easily identify you but at the same time it should include a keyword of what your interests are. If you have a brand, USE IT—it will only reinforce it. Using your first and last name is also very common, as well as using the name of your company.

The next step after signing up is to find people that you want to follow. There are several ways. One is to use the 'Find People' search option. Another option is to follow your colleagues; this will certainly increase your network. A third option is to browse and start following people whose profile description relates to you and what you are looking for.

The next step is to engage in conversations, first through @ messages and, later on, if that person follows you back, then through DMs as well. As you follow more people, you will start receiving news and trends that interest you and that can facilitate conversations.

To receive messages on Twitter, you have to follow users. Your messages will be received by your followers, not by who you follow. Answer and comment on tweets that interest you or that catch your attention. Retweet 'RT' messages that you believe your followers will be interested in; by doing so, you are sharing information that you think is important and deserves to be shared with your followers.

If you have a relevant message not only for your followers but also for followers of people that you are following, use '@username'. If that person is not following you, your message will show up in his mentions folder, and people following you and that person will also get to see the message. In addition, it will show up in search results.

Private messages should only be sent using the direct message option 'DM'. You can only DM people who are following you, and you can only receive DMs from people you are following.

Twitter functionality is limited if you use your browser. There are other platforms like HootSuite and TweetDeck that will help you enjoy your Twitter experience more and enable you to get the most out of it.You will learn more about top Twitter tools to use in Chapter 6.

Important Rules of Twitter

Twitter is a social network and some rules are important:

- When reporting events, either use links, videos, or photos; they will be more real and engaging.
- Give credit to people who deserve it. If you are sharing information you found, tell people where you found it or who wrote it.
- Be personal. Let people know who you are, what you like, your hobbies, where you work, etc.
- Be constant and participate. The more you do, the more you will be valued.
- Become an influencer and provide valuable information while tweeting.
- Do not share confidential information, do not spread rumors, and do not criticise.
- Engage in conversations, re-tweets and messages. Do not only post things about you or your company. Be natural and be yourself.
- Space your tweets; no one wants to see a full list of tweets from the same person, one after theother.

Twitter Terms That You Need to Know

The Twitter phenomenon has given rise to a whole set of terms related to Twittering. Here is a list with definitions of the most frequently used and important terms you should know.

- **@reply**: This indicates you are replying to an update sent from a specific username. Keep in mind that this does not make the tweet you send private. To do that, send it via direct message.

- **280 character limit**: Updates are meant to be brief and to-the-point. Initially a feature chosen to be compatible with SMS messaging, the character limit has played an important role in shaping the culture of Twitter.

- **DM**: Direct message, equivalent to an email, with a 280-character limit. These may be sent to anyone following you. Twitter blocks users from sending DMs to those not following them as a way to limit spam.

- **Drunktwittering/Dweet**: When Jack Daniels, or one of his relatives, takes control of your Twittering!

- **Failwhale**: The beloved bird-borne whale logo that appears when Twitter crashes. It doesn't happen often or last long, but you will see this logo occasionally.

- **Feed**: The posts you receive are commonly referred to as your Twitter feed.

- **Followers**: Folks who hang on your every tweet ... or at least receive them into their timeline.

- **GET username**: Retrieves the tweet most recently sent from that user.

- **Hashtags**: Hashtags are abbreviations which denote groupings of popular subjects. You may follow any hashtag designation you want at 'hashtag.org' to keep up with the real-time updates for that subject.

- **Microblog**: A term used to describe the Twitter platform, which is a unique blend of blogging and instant messaging.

- **Mistweet**: A tweet you'll regret later. You may delete tweets you've sent on your profile page, but unless you can get every one of your followers to delete them, they are out there for good. Think twice before you tweet!

- **NUDGE username:** Used to remind someone you are following to update.

- **Off-Twitter**: Like "offline", it means a conversation might best be moved to private channels, or that someone wants to say something privately.

- **RT/Retweet**: To retweet is to post someone's update you found enjoyable, helpful, or noteworthy. Give them credit by using the form RT #usernameyouarerequotingfrom, then quote the original. That way, a reader of your RT who wants to follow the originator will be able to do so.

- **Search**: At search.twitter.com you may search tweets by specific keyword. Twitter.com/invitations/find_on_twitter will allow you to search by name, which is also accessed with the "Find People" tab.

- **TinyURL, (https://tinyurl.com)**: The most popular URL shortening service, which snips URLs to a shorter number of characters to make them fit within the post limitations.

Twitter is a powerful social media tool. Use it wisely and you will see a return on your time invested. Happy tweeting!

Chapter 6: Marketing with Twitter

Twitter can be a powerful marketing tool that, if used correctly, can be effective in providing the same or even more income than your current full-time career. Twitter allows you to share a small fragment of your thoughts and opinions at the exact moment that it occurs with anyone that has opted in to follow your tweets. It's no wonder the catchphrase on the Twitter sign-up page is, "What Are You Doing?" Twitter can be summed up as a combination of Facebook, instant messaging and SMS, all rolled into one simple yet brilliant package.

Your tweets, along with those of the people that you are following, are all displayed on a single page immediately after it's tweeted. Your Twitter page is a constantly updated stream of news from yourself and everyone that you have opted in to "follow". That does not mean that all of your followers will receive your tweets; only those that have followed you will receive your tweets.

Therefore, if you are interested in creating a huge Twitter community with a loyal audience, you must keep your tweets engaging, funny and informative. Give your audience what they want. Keep in mind that although Twitter is an online social media tool, it is filled with millions of real people from all walks of life that are interested in finding solutions, being entertained, or are just looking for ways to keep in touch with their long-lost friends.

You might be thinking, "Wow, big deal," but there is massive potential in this mini social networking site to meet other like-minded people, share info and website links, and promote products and businesses. And those factors, combined with the ability to gain thousands of followers, make it a perfect platform for business.

Advantages of Using Twitter for Marketing

The advantage of using Twitter is its ability to quickly send a short text message to a group that can quickly be seen, discussed, and replied to. Think of it as text messaging on your phone to your entire phonebook. And just as you wouldn't want someone sending advertisements all day by phone text messages, the same applies to Twitter.

Since the flow of "tweets" can show as conversation from you for potential customers or clients to get to your website, it ends up being a time flow of updates 24 hours per day, seven days per week. Short and easy-to-read messages that people can follow let them know what is going on at that time, as well as see if you are adjusting and making offers on what they may be looking for compared to a prior post.

Twitter allows you to share pictures or graphics to catch your followers' eye better and draw them to the current updates that lead them back to your website. Keeping updated comments or offers going can keep them interested and following you. They often will leave favorable comments or constructive criticism that you can track. It allows you to make rapid advertising adjustments for what you can offer or communicate with them, and keep up with what the public is looking for from your business. This is real-time public supply and demand through communication, and real time-sensitive offers that lead people to your site and business highlights.

Twitter allows for third-party developers to manipulate your application programme interface (API) and install applications on your Twitter page to enhance its capabilities. APIs not only add the Twitter widget to your website but can link people from Twitter to you at your website. This is compatible with many other social media network sites as well, all stemming from and drawing followers to what you want potential clients and customers to see in your current offerings and website content.

Twitter is the most used and respected online social media tool in the world and has quickly become a goldmine for many business owners and entrepreneurs. If you are not yet a member, sign up and find out what all of the fuss is about.

Chapter 7: 25 New Ideas for Social Media Marketing Using Twitter

As communications is a key feature of Twitter, marketing products and services via Twitter could be the secret to a marketer's success. With viral marketing being the buzzword in marketing circles, Twitter can be exploited to its full potential as a viral marketing tool. Explained in this chapter are 25 unique ideas you can use to market your products and services via Twitter.

Idea #1: Become Attractive

What I mean by becoming attractive is, remember to use the rules of attraction marketing and be sure to provide content and value. If your niche market is other network marketers, then your content (blog posts, updates and articles) shouldn't be about anything other than topics that pertain to leadership or the industry. There's nothing worse than going to someone's site and not being able to pinpoint exactly what they do. When you provide a link in your tweets, you want the information to be so useful that it becomes worth retweeting or goes viral.

Idea #2: Stand Out

How do you stand out? Do what everyone else is NOT doing. If you haven't noticed, everyone is selling or promoting something on Twitter. In order to avoid getting lost in the crowd, build relationships instead of selling. There may be millions of tweets out there, but many people are looking to make a worthwhile connection with you. Would you do business with someone that only looked at you as a dollar sign? I would hope not.

Idea #3: Engage Your CEO in Social Media

Social media is an excellent way to have a conversation with your market, make connections, and manage those connections with customers, prospects, bloggers, etc. However, for a CEO, the characteristic routes to social media can be tough, especially with larger companies. Generally, a CEO doesn't have time to write a blog, answer a bunch of messages, or deal with tons of friend requests on Facebook.

Twitter is a method that eliminates all those hassles. It's quick and easy. Twitter is limited to 280 characters per update, so it is all about short thoughts and comments. If you can send a text message, you can use Twitter from anywhere in the world as a marketing tool.

Idea #4: Keep Your Followers Intrigued... Be Creative

The quickest way for someone to "unfollow" you is to repeat the same tweet, over and over and over and over ... get my point? Be creative, keep your readers intrigued, and be original! Maybe you can write your tweets in story form one day or in a poetic rhyme—whatever it is, keep them following. With Twitter usage growing leaps and bounds on a daily basis, you must fight to get noticed. Make your 280 characters work for you! Yes, there are only 280 characters (not words), so make them as powerful as 280,000 characters. The power is in your tweet.

Idea #5: Build Your List

It's nice to tweet quotes and other empowering notes, but one of the main reasons you're on Twitter is to build an effective following. Every day there should be a tweet including a link that leads traffic to your blog or affiliate site; if not, then you're just wasting time.

In order for your ecommerce business to build followers on the social channel you choose, you must entice customers with something they aren't able to get anywhere else. Offer an exclusive item to social media followers or fans, such as a weekly coupon. You might also offer "breaking news" that they can't find somewhere else.

Idea #6: Promote Webinars, Blog Articles, News, Etc.

It's really easy to post a link on Twitter. Share valuable information through your tweets. You not only promote your name and business, you get to share to thousands of people who could retweet your information to their own followers!

People love reading interesting articles, news items, and web-based seminars. You can post a link on Twitter to redirect followers to your website. The same can be done on other websites which have some relevance to the kind of business that you do. Content that is interesting to your audiences will make it very easy for you to make money online by getting them to the right place where you have your products or services they can buy. This, however, means taking time to choose the content to include in the article to hold the attention of the viewers to the very last word. It can be frustrating when there is attraction, but interest is lost along the way.

Idea #7: Announce Specials, Sales, or Deals

If you often have special offers, you can use Twitter to instantly broadcast these deals. If you have some exciting promotional activities, Twitter is a nifty way of getting the message across to your target market. Remember, though, that Twitter should not be used as a pitch tool. This turns people off, so you don't want to be doing any aggressive marketing here because this should be a place for sharing information and knowledge.

Idea #8: Don't Just Promote Products/Services

The main focus of your ecommerce site is to sell products, but your social media marketing strategy should include a wide range of strategies that go beyond promotional offerings. Here are a few ideas to try incorporating into your social media marketing.

- Share news stories or messages from external sources
- Create a blog on your site, then feed your blog content to your social media accounts
- Ask questions, poll your customers, or participate in discussions via social media
- Post pictures from company events or videos, especially when the CEO speaks

Idea #9: Monitor What Your Competitors Are Doing

Whether your ecommerce business is new to social media marketing, or you just want to take it up a notch, competitive intelligence can be very helpful. Conduct a competitive audit of your top five competitors on the social web and then answer the following questions.

- What social sites are they active on?
- What type of content do they publish?
- How many followers/views/fans do they have on their site?
- How do they promote their products, events, or programmes using social media?

Idea #10: Keep in Touch With Bloggers/Media

Bloggers abound on Twitter. Follow those who inspire you, and find others who have valuable information to share too. Be friends, and take advantage of the power of the retweet button to spread great information!

If you look at Twitter from a personal-brand-building and networking standpoint, you will realise that you should NOT look at microblogging as individual posts, as you may think they can be useless. Instead, think of the overall impressions and value that can be created by using Twitter for marketing over time.

Idea #11: Automation

One or two tweets just won't do. Unless you have a lot of time on your hands and can update on a regular basis, I advise you to "automate" your tweets. Sites like Hootsuite, TweetDeck and Social Oomph, to name a few, help keep you tweeting throughout the day. Set aside time in the evening or morning, whatever works best for you, and load your greetings (Social Oomph) and tweets for the day. Automated tweeting is like having a virtual social media assistant. Be sure to check these sites daily for direct mentions (when someone tweets about you) and direct messages that need your response.

Idea #12: Monitor Your Company or Brand on Twitter

By monitoring, you'll be able to tell what's working and what's not and make the necessary changes. You can also monitor what people are saying about any person, topic or company. Twitter has a search engine that lets you do just that. Or, you can use the hashtag (# symbol).

Be professional in your approach. Treat people with the respect that they deserve. Communicate as much as you can. Communicating does not only mean posting tweet after tweet. It also means sitting back and reading what your readers have to say and then reverting.

Idea #13: Listen to Your Target Market

With simple tweets, you can actually learn from what they want and what they prefer. Tweets can be a good feedback system where people can air their comments and feedback and you can take advantage of that as part of your market research.

Idea #14: Show Appreciation

Show your appreciation where it's due. If you like something that was written by one of your customers or readers, be lavish in your approbation. Believe me, appreciation is one of the strongest Twitter marketing tools that you can use to improve public relations. Take interest in people and they will take interest in you.

Idea #15: Sponsor Contests, Polls or Giveaways

Sponsor contests and polls, or give away freebies with your tweets. Of course, small marketing efforts like this can become viral on social networks and can be your way of engaging your potential customers and online followers, helping you to gain more of them and make your business more known.

Idea #16: Use Keywords in Your Tweets

Keywords are important tools online to let your ads, your website, or your content be seen by the people as well as the search engines. Of course, you have to remember that you are not only marketing your products and your business to online readers but you also aim to be indexed by search engines, which will make your website visible to more people who are looking for it.

Idea #17: Don't Transform Twitter into a Purpose

It's very tempting to transform your tweeting campaign into a reason. What you need to remember at all times is that Twitter should only serve as a tool. This means that all the strategies you put into practice should have an end result of drawing more earnings towards you. At all times, you need to be considering your tweets in terms of profit and eventual increase in your sales. Thus, just bear in mind—Twitter is a means!

Idea #18: Don't Pull Towards People Who Are Not Really Fascinating

It's very persuasive to worry about all sorts of groups once you're on Twitter. You are motivated to talk to everyone and persuade them all to tag along with you. However, you're wasting your time if you influence people to follow you simply for the following itself. Keep in mind that the community you target should be an area of people who are fond of your stuff and are likely to invest.

Idea #19: Don't Spam!

Simply put, do not spam. Only use Twitter when you have something new and attractive to tell people. Use ads and discounts to build it chill and tweetable. Just don't grow to be the sort of addict who keeps twittering without composing something a little helpful to say! Never spam is the most important law in learning how to use Twitter for marketing.

Idea #20: Don't Turn Out to Be Impersonal

Bear in mind always that you are tweeting by means of a social platform. You are talking to people and look forward to people, not machines. So place in individual information and remarks while you tweet. Formulate your tweets in a human-centred way.

Idea #21: Build a Network

Use Twitter to build up a network because that is the whole purpose of social networking. The platform is a perfect place to build up your authority. Your authority is a great way to guide people to free information to learn, but if they want to find out more, they will have to make a purchase. You brand yourself so people trust you.

You can do keyword-related searches on Twitter Search and then follow users who might be interested in what you sell or the services you offer. In turn, many of these people will follow you and you can begin marketing to them by tweeting about topics related to your product or service.

Idea #22: Tweet Regularly

In order to build up followers on Twitter, you need to tweet often so that people can keep track of what you are doing. When you are practising internet marketing for your affiliate marketing business, you need to make sure you continue to update your followers on the latest developments in your business with Twitter.

Idea #23: Build Credibility

Being engaged in the online community and offering helpful insights, tips and content to your followers will help you gain trust and credibility with your customer base. Done right, Twitter will help you showcase your industry knowledge and expertise.

Idea #24: Live Updates on Events

Whether you have corporate events or trade shows you participate in, you can use Twitter to announce the event, reveal last-minute changes, and more. It is an excellent last-minute marketing tool.

Idea #25: Think Success

If you present yourself as being successful in your internet marketing on Twitter, you will be perceived as being successful. This is not the venue to underplay your hand. The more of a success you are, the more others will want to follow.

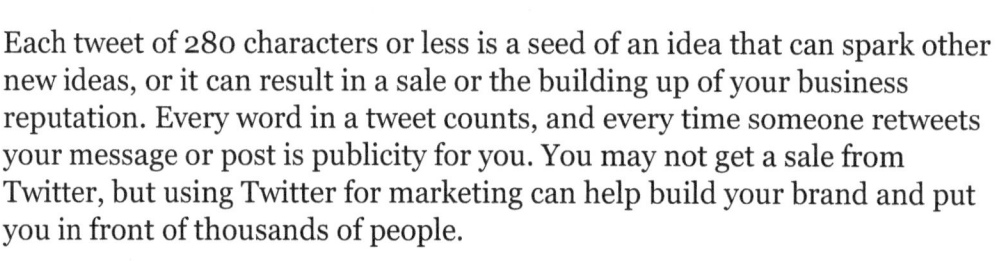

Each tweet of 280 characters or less is a seed of an idea that can spark other new ideas, or it can result in a sale or the building up of your business reputation. Every word in a tweet counts, and every time someone retweets your message or post is publicity for you. You may not get a sale from Twitter, but using Twitter for marketing can help build your brand and put you in front of thousands of people.

Indeed, Twitter is a great promotional and marketing tool, and not just for pointing to interesting things you've found on the web. It's great for building credibility and influence, so use it, and use it well.

Chapter 8: Understanding the Playing Field of Social Media Marketing

Designing and building a social media campaign that's successful is a bit like designing and building a high-rise. First, you need to research your material, then you need to put down a solid foundation, and then you need to continue with regular maintenance to ensure your social media promotion is a success.

- **The Proper Building Blocks**

The proper building blocks are key to successful social media marketing. The strongest social media plan needs to include the following building blocks:

- **Democratized Social News Sites**

These tools permit online marketers to network with a community by both voting on content and by submitting your own content for others to vote on. Examples include Reddit and Mixx.

- **Social Sites**

These sites offer a fantastic opportunity to build and interact with a network, and to publish your original content in a number of forms such as videos, photos, links, news, and more. Examples include Facebook and LinkedIn.

- **Editor-Controlled News Sites**

When content the user submits fits the editorial guidelines, it is accepted and distributed. These high-profile websites can produce enormous results. Yahoo is a great example of a news site.

- **Microblogging Sites**

These include sites like Twitter and Friendfeed, where your comments are limited to 280 characters or less. Keep your comments interesting. It's a great way to broadcast to a large audience.

- **Social Bookmarking Sites**

Social bookmarking sites are a great tool for marketers. You can submit URLs of interest to sites like Delicious.com and StumbleUpon.com which will drive targeted traffic to a specific page. These sites are great for doing research relating to the type of content that your audience is interested in.

- **Wiki Sites**

If you want to dominate search results, wikis are a great tool, because they frequently rank high. Use wikis to reach new audiences by posting original content and editing existing content.

- **Social Question and Answer Sites**

Marketers can answer existing questions and post new questions on sites such as Wiki Answers and Yahoo! Answers. This is a great way to develop and grow brand reputation and become an authority. It's also an excellent way to do audience research.

- **Social Content Sharing Sites**

Flickr and YouTube are just a couple of the sites that let you post specific content types, from photos to video to reviews. These sites can aid marketers to build brand recognition and to target relevant audiences.

- **Niche Sites**

These sites target a specific niche, such as Chihuahuas, Italian wine, or blogging. As a marketer, these are excellent because you are able to target an extremely relevant audience.

In order to create a social media campaign that will be successful, you must have a detailed plan. These steps will ensure your campaign is solid.

- **Background Research**

Learn where your online audience is located. Examine the type of content they submit to social media sites for ideas of what interests them. Also, identify thought leaders to target in order to spread your message to a broad audience.

- **Brainstorming**

The purpose of brainstorming is to generate tons of ideas that you can use for promotions. Have a look at what has worked in the past and then build upon that. Look at what has worked for other similar companies or products and then see how that could be integrated into your platform. Take the time to filter out the good, the bad, and the really good, so that you can find a workable solution.

- **Idea Research**

You will need to follow up on the ideas you implemented to see if they actually worked (and how well they worked) based on what is currently happening in the targeted social media. Flexibility is really important, as is the ability to adapt and change if something isn't right. After all, there's no point in continuing down a path that isn't working.

- **Story Production**

Work hard to avoid a message that is an obvious sales pitch, and what's referred to as marketing speak. Use videos and photos to enrich your stories.

- **Schedule and Launch**

You need to be aware of the days and the times you targeted audience is on the social network sites. Make sure you link your promotions to relevant events to generate timely interest.

- **Build a Foundation**

For your social media marketing campaign to be a success it's key to interact with a social community and build a strong foundation. There's a reason it's called social. Make sure you are socialising with an appropriate community and use these guidelines to get the most out of your campaign.

- **Network and Be Social**

You should continuously join and participate in groups, make new friends and interact with existing friends, and in general participate in the community.

- **Be Genuine and On Target**

Provide your audience with what it wants.

- **Provide Value**

Provide users with something of value—expert advice, tips, something entertaining, etc.

- **Allow People to Act Naturally**

Allow users to have fun with your content and interact in a natural way. Don't force them to interact in a specific manner.

- **Listen and Respond**

Watch for positive and negative reactions to your content once it goes live. Respond to your users and always work to improve content.

Go Where You'll Find Your Customers

Digital and social media marketing offer endless options. From Facebook to LinkedIn to Twitter to YouTube, there is an endless array of social networking channels available that your business can leverage. The key to winning social media ecommerce marketing is to choose the right channels so you reach customers.

You can learn where your customers gather by:

- **Asking them**. While it sounds simple, it's often overlooked. Just send out a formal survey to customers or do an informal poll on your website, which can provide a wealth of knowledge.
- **Monitoring social sites**. There are a number of free tools such as Trackur.com to learn how and where customers are talking about your competitors, your brand, or your target keywords. There are also paid programmes that are more robust.
- **Leveraging the stats**. When it comes to stats, some sites like Facebook are transparent or you can leverage third-party research.

Review job postings, backlinks, keyword rankings of competitors, and news announcements regularly to get a quick look into your online marketing health.

Social Media for E-Commerce Marketing

If you run an ecommerce business, chances are your customers are active on social networks regardless of their gender, age, or economic status. Recent trends show us that both B2Cs and B2Bs are using social media for ecommerce. Facebook, for example, is huge and is expected to continue growing. In a recent study, more than 89 percent of small business owners are using Facebook and 68 percent of them say that Facebook is the social media tool they use the most. In addition, 77.5 percent say they will spend even more on social media.

According to the study, these are the top reasons that small businesses are choosing social media:

- 40.8% – to attract new customers
- 27.6% – to promote their brand
- 15.7% – to communicate company news via social sites
- 11.3% – to stay in touch with existing customers

Many ecommerce sites use social channels to make it easier for customers to purchase their products. For example, 1-800-Flowers was the first ecommerce site to launch a Facebook store, which allowed customers to browse and purchase its products directly through Facebook.

Some businesses are actually using Twitter to respond to complaints that their customers have tweeted. Dell increased sales by more than 1 million in 2009 doing just that. When a customer is contacted in real time it shows that the business cares and will make the effort to effectively communicate and correct any issues or problems.

Because the internet is an integral part of our lives, we have become accustomed to instant or quick responses to our problems. Businesses that respond in real time to their customers will surely grow customer loyalty. Staying competitive in today's market means being flexible and utilising social media in customer relations.

The Wrong Way to Use Social Media Marketing

When it comes to generating results in their social media marketing campaigns, some social media marketers choose to cross over to the dark side... and we're not talking about Darth Vader's dark side. Avoid creating a social media ring so members can vote your content up, messing with the reputation of a competitor, using social media applications that automate processes, or hacking WordPress blogs to include your link. Avoid these unscrupulous tactics because they will not benefit you over the long haul and can actually jeopardise your long-term success.

Create a comprehensive social media campaign by putting focusing on the three major stages we talked about: 1. Proper building blocks, 2. Blueprint, and 3. Building a foundation.

Social media marketing is a powerful tool, so make sure you get the most out of it.☐

Chapter 9: Top Twitter Tools to Use

There are all kinds of valuable Twitter tools you should know about to get the most out of your Twitter social media marketing experience. Let's have a look at the top ten.

1. Buffer

It is truly easier to throw your daily content into a bucket and then have an application automatically do the posting work for you. Depending on how heavy a user you are and how many social media accounts you plan to run, there is both a free and paid version.

Cost: Free and paid versions.

2. HootSuite

HootSuite is an excellent tool to help keep your social networking organised. I use it daily as the platform to launch all of my tweets, Facebook posts, and LinkedIn updates. It offers both a robust free version and a paid version. Both provide the ability to shrink links down (ow.ly), publish posts for later, organise lists into groups, do easy profile research, and analytics. Additionally, HootSuite offers a team feature to allow groups of individuals the ability to keep track of what is set up to go out and what has successfully been viewed.

Cost: Free and paid versions

3. TwitterCounter

TwitterCounter offers basic analytics and graphs on things like followers and tweets. It has a sorting feature by hourly or monthly. It also produces real-time statistics and creates content on this for your followers automatically.

Cost: Free version and premium version

4. TweetDeck

Much like Hootsuite, TweetDeck is a dashboard management tool which gives users the ability to organise their Twitter and other social media accounts into easier-to-view and -understand columns. It is an application owned by Twitter, not a third-party provider. The biggest benefit of TweetDeck is its ability to organise your Twitter audience into groups which can make it easier to create customised marketing communication.

Cost: Free

5. SocialOomph

SocialOomph is a Twitter tool that provides a long list of services, including auto-following. It also allows you to create a handful of automated reply messages to those who follow you. It will randomly choose a reply from your group of replies so that things don't feel so ... automated. Finally, it allows you to schedule tweets for the future at any date, time and frequency.

COST: There is a free version and a version which costs about $8 per month

6. SocialBro

A nearly all-in-one platform for all things Twitter. The free plan comes with analytics, best time to tweet, follow/unfollow tools, and community segmentation.

Cost: Free and paid versions

7. Tweriod

If you want a Twitter tool which can review your account activity and give you recommendations on the best times to send your tweets to maximise your followers' clicks, this is that tool. It is completely free and takes minutes. Once it has an analysis, it sends an email with the full report.

Cost: Free for basic analysis. The premium analysis starts at $2.50.

8. TweetAdder

If you are looking to add Twitter followers fast, this may be the tool for you. It is said it can easily add up to 150 new like-minded followers to your account every day. TweetAdder is a software application which allows you to automatically build followers, send replies and thank-yous, and current and future-date messages. This Twitter tool is not a web application, but rather, it is loaded onto your computer.

Cost: You must purchase the software. It is a one time purchase of $55–$180 depending on your needs.

9. Riffle

This browser plugin reveals vast insights into any Twitter user you choose. Discover statistics, popular hashtags, most shared links, connected profiles, and much more.

Cost: Free and paid versions

Chapter 10: The 5 S's of Social Media Marketing

It's important for you to understand the social aspect of how users utilise social media sites to adapt and be a success at their business. Social media revolves around social networking sites. Let's look at the 5 S's of social media marketing your business should utilise.

Share

Social media is all about sharing. Individuals write blogs for the world to read, upload videos to sites like YouTube for the world to see, share bookmarks with sites like Digg, and post links to points of interest on Twitter. If your goal is to explore social media marketing and venture out, it's important to recognise the conversations can't be all about you or your company. Share information about your company with the rest of the world through social media and show your audience your company has the necessary expertise.

For example, with Twitter, the recommended formula is 10 percent sharing to 20 percent self-advertising. Of course, the formula isn't set in stone, so experiment and see what works best.

Support

When you think about it, social media is pretty fantastic because users are having real-time conversations about anything and everything you can think of. PR agencies are beginning to strongly recommend that companies keep a social media presence. Social media sites like Twitter allow an avenue for customer support.

Social

Social media is about socialising with existing friends and making new friends. For your social media marketing to be successful, you need to interact with your followers who are your potential customers. Socialising and growing your fan base increases your presence. Think of social media as virtual socialisation and for your business, it is a virtual marketing mecca. Engage + communicate + socialize = successful social media marketing.

Strategy

Make sure you have a social media marketing strategy in place. Otherwise, you could be wasting a great deal of time and money. Each social media type has a different environment, functionality, and demographic base. Determine what it is you want to achieve using social media, then analyse the different social media types and the various channels each offers. Create your online profile, brand your products/services, and then execute your plan. Make sure you analyse the effectiveness of your marketing strategy and make any needed changes. Social media is fluid and constantly changing, so you may have to fine-tune your strategy as things change.

Sales

All the social media marketing campaigns are of no value to you and your business if they don't generate sales for you. You need to be creative. Set up a landing page, craft unique product campaigns, make pages trackable so you have access to data, and do anything else you can to track how effective your social media campaign is.

There you have it: The 5 S's that can make your social media marketing campaign a success.

Chapter 11: Ten Commandments to Maximise Your SMM Campaign

Commandments #1: Thou Shall Blog Like Crazy

Blog. Please. That's the first priority. Set up a blog, a personal blog, a business blog. It's easier than you think. Use an existing blogging site such as Blogger.com or GOingOn.com, or install your own branded blogging site right on your own server by using WordPress. And, WordPress is free.

Commandments #2: Thou Shall Create Thine Profiles

Create your profiles sooner rather than later because if someone else takes them, they are gone forever. This is referred to as cybersquatting. So, get busy—get out there now and start creating your profiles. You can use Open Social to make the filling out of each profile as easy as one, two, three, and a click of a button.

Commandments #3: Thou Shall Upload Lots of Photos

Upload as many good photographs as you have. Now this doesn't mean you should be uploading pictures of you dancing on a tabletop wearing a lampshade, as these types of photographs will hurt you rather than help you. Customers and potential customers want to see photographs of your company in action and you participating. Your audience wants to put a face to your company.

Commandments #4: Thou Shall Podcast Often

You can use the free audio software on your computer or invest in a relatively cheap camera. Podcasts can run 24 hours a day. Once you've created your podcasts, there's no cost associated with providing them to your customers and potential customers, and they offer a great deal of value in building your business. Do interviews, training lessons, and any other type of podcast that is interesting, entertaining, and relevant.

Commandments #5: Thou Shall Upload All the Videos You Can Find

Post videos, more videos, and then some more videos. They can be customer videos, training videos, or entertaining videos. So, grab the video camera, get out there, and start interviewing customers and anyone else that can provide valuable information. Pictures are worth a thousand words, and a happy customer smiling is just that.

Commandments #6: Thou Shall Immediately Set Alerts

Alerts are a must. When people are talking about you and your business, you want to be alerted as to what they are saying and when they are saying it. This information can be useful in creating powerful social media campaigns.

Commandments #7: Thou Shall Get Connected With Everyone

Get connected by signing up to LinkedIn, Facebook, Twitter, and other social media sites. On your email signature put that you have a LinkedIn, Facebook, and Twitter account. Also include it on your business cards, on your letterhead, and anywhere else where there is an opportunity to promote your social media presence.

Commandments #8: Thou Shall Comment on a Multitude of Blogs

Commenting on blogs is a bit like having a chat at a cocktail party or other type of event. Just as you would not walk into a cocktail party or event, walk up to a group that's chatting, and tell them your name and your business, you shouldn't do it on a blog. Posting a comment on a blog is fine but you don't want to come across as rude. So first listen by reading the posts and then make a comment post. It's okay to be controversial or voice your opinion even if it doesn't agree with the poster's opinion, but you must do it in a manner that's respectful. There's a great opportunity here to promote your business, so don't miss out on it.

Commandments #9: Thou Shall Explore Social Media for a Minimum of 30 Minutes Per Week

Every week, you should explore social media for at least 30 minutes. Of course, longer is better. So, why not grab a cup of java, park yourself in front of your computer for 30 minutes, and start searching? Using the Google search engine is an effective way to search for and find social media sites. This is also a good way to look at expanding into other social media sites.

Commandments #10: Thou Shall Be Creative

Of all the commandments, this is by far the most important. Have some fun and let your creativity flow. Know what your customers want and expect and then provide that to them in a manner that catches their attention. Remember your audience wants transparency, authenticity, to be able to communicate openly, and to have a little fun.

These ten commandments will guide you in your quest for maximising your social media marketing.□

Chapter 12: The Future of Twitter Marketing

According to Mark Schaefer, who is an important consultant in marketing, it was predicted that Twitter would be reborn and transformed, and will be an essential player in the field of marketing. His reasons are because there are some positive signs in the growth of the users and the income to Twitter.

Also, there is a massive and committed public of around 330 million people. That audience places Twitter as the alternative advertising option to Facebook, Instagram, and Adwords. Below, we'll analyse Twitter's various new features that we look forward to seeing.

Status Updates

During an event at CES in early 2019, Twitter detailed new features that could drastically change the way people share and talk to one another on its platform.

The updates include a new design for threads, meant to make it easier to follow conversations as they unfold, as well as completely new features like statuses and presence indicators that could indicate when someone is online or when someone is typing.

Twitter will start to test these experimental features "in the coming weeks publicly," when it launches a beta program for people who want to participate in the tests. It's a relatively new approach for Twitter to experiment so openly, but the company says all the features are geared toward its bigger goal of improving "conversational health" on the platform.

At first glance, features like status updates or presence indicators showing you're "online" sound much more like what you'd expect from Facebook, not Twitter. But Twitter's director of product management, Sara Haider, says the changes are meant to give people more flexibility. Adding a dedicated status update feature would add more context to tweets, and avoid the need for workarounds like changing your display name, she said.

Improved Conversations

Another big focus, Haider said, is trying to make conversations easier for people to follow. Right now, it can be a struggle to follow long threads with many different replies because replies often appear out of order and you need to do a lot of tapping around in the app to detangle a conversation.

To solve that, the company is testing new designs for replies that would thread tweets together in a way that looks more similar to comments on a Reddit post. In one prototype Twitter is testing, discussions that branch off from a reply to a single tweet would instead be nested, making it more clear who is talking to whom.

"We've spent a lot of time on making sure that people can find what they're looking for when something is unfolding in real time. We're now asking ourselves the question, how do we make this experience even deeper and richer, so we decided to focus on conversations," she explained.

During the CES event, Twitter's VP of product, Keith Coleman, identified health as the company's top product priority for the coming year.

"Health is our number one priority, hands down. We know that to serve our company's purpose, we need that conversation to be healthy," he said, noting that Twitter has made 70 changes to its product and policies over the last year to weed out abuse.

Video Content Will Be the King

Carmen Collins is the leader in social media of the famous Cisco agency, and she predicted something that we are experiencing every day. Collins said videos are flooding all social networks.

In fact, the "Stories" are born by the demand of people to be able to share their life in short and simple videos. For brands, it won't be enough to create a video. They must also publish that audiovisual content in the most channels to achieve maximum exposure.

Artificial Intelligence (AI)

In the coming years, AI is sure to touch everything we do. But let's focus on what will affect marketers the most.

As Futurist Kevin Kelly writes, innovation will come in the form of applying a layer of AI over our everyday tasks. This will make tasks quicker, more accurate, more integrated, and more personal, ushering in the "Age of Assistance".

Companies will rise or fall based on how cleverly they can apply layers of AI to give their customers experiences that are helpful, exciting and entertaining.

If you're struggling to keep up with these trends and are looking for a fresh approach, feel free to call your friendly Mediaplanet office for a chat today. We'll help you navigate the changes and create content that delivers on your business objectives.

Now, everything we have discussed here is just a prediction. But of course, there are those who indicate the opposite.

In Forbes, Mark Gale, who is also a specialist in strategic communication and marketing, headlines a note that reads: "Why Twitter is not the future of marketing." Let's see the reasons. (Of course, Mark Gale is not the only one who thinks that Twitter does not have much of a future as it is seen now):

Twitter has a very flat growth curve. It is no longer an instant news source. Now there are other ways to find out what are the events of the day quickly. With the possibility of creating groups on Facebook (in addition to other options on other platforms), the "tribes" have left Twitter. It is no longer an indicated space for traction or engagement.

Mark added, "As a business owner, the personal value that Twitter gives me continues to decline. The domain of celebrities has made Twitter more a megaphone for celebrities and less useful to me as an information and communication tool. Twitter once connected me directly with my colleagues and with information that I could not get anywhere else. It does not do that anymore."

Conclusion

Again, I want to thank you for downloading this book and I hope you will be able to use it to grow your brand and improve your social media marketing with some new strategies for growth.

Social media has taken the world by storm, and social media marketing by tweeting via Twitter is all the rage these days. Businesses that recognise this and the power of this virtual world are taking advantage of the opportunity to grow and prosper using social media marketing. Don't be afraid to reach out and use many different social media channels and venues. We've discussed many in this ebook, but there are plenty of others. We've pointed you in the right direction—now get busy and expand on the information we've provided.

Social media makes it easy for you to target the appropriate audience. There's little value in targeting the wrong audience. For example, if you are selling adult entertainment, you wouldn't want to target a family audience. Be patient, and take the necessary time to determine which channels will best benefit your business.

Twitter has quickly become famous, utilised by everyone from tech-savvy corporate types to people sending out an SOS in third-world countries. The idea of sending short 280-character messages to a list of followers has become more and more popular. With Twitter being one of the dominant social media sites in the world, using a good strategy is crucial in your social media marketing.

Make sure to keep tweeting a few times a day to build a loyal following. You don't need to spend hours; just a few minutes here and there is enough to find and post useful information. Start using Twitter daily with the methods and strategies discussed and make it an essential part of your social media marketing campaign.

Generally, for your social media campaigns, you should join groups, like pages, and interact as much as possible. The more you interact and engage in discussion, the more your following will grow and the more your business will prosper. Your comments and discussions should offer information that's relevant and interesting. Posting just to post will annoy your audience, which is not what you want to do.

You can start slowly so that you don't become overwhelmed. Facebook is a good place to start, followed by Twitter and YouTube. Once you've created your profiles and set up your page(s), you are ready to begin to enjoy all the benefits that social media has to offer. It won't take you long at all to put your plan into action, especially if you make use of the valuable information we've provided you.

Marketing is key to the success of any business. Those businesses that recognise the power of social media marketing will be miles ahead of the competition. So are you ready to take your business to new levels? Are you ready to jump-start your client base? And are you ready to share with others just how you were able to become so successful? Because they are going to be asking. The secret is yours to keep for as long as you like.

Finally, if you enjoyed this book, then I'd like to ask you for a favour: Would you be kind enough to leave a review here: **https://www.amazon.com/product-reviews/B07PFXJRCG** for this book on Amazon? It'd be greatly appreciated!

Thank you and good luck!

Robert Awere